Contents

Words that appear in **bold** in the text are explained in the glossary.

Your neighbourhood

Wherever you live in Britain, there is a huge variety of trees and wild flowers to discover in your neighbourhood.

Finding flowers

Flowering plants have existed on Earth for around 160 million years and grow almost anywhere. Grassy meadows and woodlands are the perfect home for many wild flowers, but you can spot them in every kind of **habitat**, from towns and cities to coasts and mountains.

Seasonal highlights

From carpets of wood anemones and bluebells to fields full of poppies and buttercups, the highlights of the wild flower year come in the spring and summer.

What are flowers?

Flowering plants belong to a group of living things called angiosperms, which means 'seed vessel'. There are between 250,000 and 400,000 species of flowering plant in the world. They all produce flowers, which develop into fruits containing seeds.

A woodland carpeted with bluebells is one of the most spectacular sights of the British countryside.

Tree types

Trees are the giants of the plant world, with tough woody trunks instead of fleshy **stems**. They can be divided into two main groups – **conifers** and **broadleaved trees**.

Flowers and cones

Broadleaved trees are a type of flowering plant. Like all angiosperms, they produce their seeds from flowers. Conifers do not have flowers. Instead, they make their seeds inside woody **cones**.

Top trees

Trees are fascinating at all times of year. In the spring, new leaves burst open on **deciduous** trees and beautiful blossom appears. In the autumn, there are colourful leaves to enjoy and a whole host of fruits to discover. Winter is a great time to see wildlife in the branches and have a close look at different kinds of bark.

Identifying flowers and trees

You can enjoy wild flowers and trees without knowing their names, but you probably know more than you think. If you see a tree or flower you don't recognise, you might want to find out what kind it is. This book will help you **identify** some of the flowers and trees you might see.

In the autumn, the leaves of most broadleaved trees change colour and fall from the trees.

Leaves and needles

Broadleaved trees usually have wide, flat leaves, while conifers have stiff, narrow **needles** or scaly leaves. Most broadleaved trees are deciduous, which means they shed all their leaves in the autumn, while most conifers are evergreen.

Trees in our cities and towns

In the hustle and bustle of life in our towns and cities, it's easy not to notice the trees. But trees breathe life into built-up areas, and once you start looking you will be amazed at how impressive they are.

Shoots and leaves

Look at all the new leaves sprouting from the bottom of this lime tree. A lime tree often has lots of leaf shoots called suckers around its base. The leaves are a bright green colour in spring. These trees can grow up to 25 m tall, but they are often cut back so they don't grow too big.

Looking at leaves

One of the first things to look at when you are trying to identify a tree is the shape of its leaves. Some broadleaved trees have leaves in a single piece. These are called simple leaves. Other trees have leaves made up of sections called leaflets. These are called compound leaves.

In the summer sunshine, lime trees bring welcome shade to many streets in Britain's towns and cities.

Common lime trees have simple heart-shaped leaves.

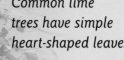

You can recognise a horse chestnut tree by its compound leaves, which have five to seven finger-like leaflets. In late spring, look out for the trees' candle-like flowers.

Bark clues

Lime trees, horse chestnuts and London planes are all deciduous trees, which lose their leaves in the autumn. One way to identify a tree when it has no leaves is to look at the texture and colour of its bark.

Conker time

Have you ever found shiny brown conkers in your local park in the autumn? These nuts are the fruits of the horse chestnut tree. Horse chestnut trees grow in parks and along roadsides in cities and towns throughout Britain.

Grime busters

One of the first things you'll notice about a London plane tree (right) is its papery bark. All tree bark is covered in very tiny holes called lenticels, which allow the tree to take in air. The holes in the bark of a London plane get clogged with dirt from the city, so the tree regularly sheds patches of bark to get rid of the grime.

You will find London planes growing in towns and cities all over Britain. These huge trees can grow up to 45 m tall and live for over 300 years.

Urban wild flowers

You don't have to live in the countryside to have wild flowers growing nearby. Many wild flowers grow in cities and towns and you won't find them hard to spot.

Dainty daisies

With their bright yellow centres and white petals, common daisies are among the easiest wild flowers to recognise. Daisies are often thought of as **weeds**, but they are a good source of sweet **nectar** for insects such as butterflies and bees.

Urban jungles

Areas of unused waste ground in cities and towns are often home to a surprising variety of wild flowers. They provide a fantastic habitat for tough flowers such as rosebay willowherb. This wild flower grows well in areas where the soil is poor and low in **nutrients**.

These purply-pink rosebay willowherb flowers (below) are growing near to a disused railway.

You can find daisies (above) in most garden lawns and parks, and no one will mind if you pick them!

Dandelions can spring up just about anywhere.

When the seeds of dandelion plants (above) float away, it helps the plants to spread far and wide.

Yellow dandelions

You are sure to know what dandelions look like. They often grow in places where they are not wanted, so they are usually regarded as weeds.

Floating away

When they have finished flowering, dandelions form fluffy, white **seed heads**. Each seed has its own 'parachute', which floats away in the wind, taking the seed with it.

Dead nettles

These white dead nettles (right) aren't actually dead! They are called 'dead' because, unlike stinging nettles (below), they won't sting you.

The leaves and stems of stinging nettles (below) are covered in tiny, stinging hairs.

A dead nettle's flowers (right) are divided into two parts, a bit like lips.

Will it sting?

You can tell stinging nettles and dead nettles apart by looking at their stems and their flowers. Dead nettles have square stems, while those of stinging nettles are round. Dead nettles have white, purple or yellow flowers. Stinging nettles have clusters of tiny green or brownish flowers that hang down in spikes.

Hedgerow trees

For hundreds of years, hedgerows have divided the countryside into a patchwork of different fields. It is easy to overlook them, but of all British habitats, hedgerows are among the most fun to explore.

May trees

Have you ever noticed how some hedgerows turn almost completely white in May? This is when hawthorn trees, also known as May trees, are in full flower. By the autumn, the trees are covered in bright red berries, called haws.

With their pretty white blossom, hawthorn trees are one of the most familiar sights in British hedgerows.

From flower to fruit

When insects visit flowers to feed on their nectar, dust-like grains of **pollen** stick to their bodies. As the insects move from bloom to bloom, they **pollinate** the flowers. After pollination, the flowers gradually develop into berries and other kinds of fruits. The fruits contain seeds, from which new plants will grow.

In the autumn and winter, birds such as blackbirds love to feast on hawthorn berries.

How old is the hedge?

When you are exploring a hedgerow, it's fun to see how many different trees you can spot. As well as hawthorns, elders and crab apples, look out for holly and hazel trees. In a 30-m stretch of an **ancient hedgerow**, it is said there will be one species of tree or woody **shrub** for every hundred years of the hedgerow's life. So if you find five species, the hedgerow could be 500 years old!

Crab apples are too sour to eat raw, but they can be made into delicious jellies.

Scented elders

As spring turns to summer, it's hard to miss the creamy-white flowers of elder trees in hedgerows. If you get close, you will smell their sweet, summery scent.

If you gently shake an elderflower, you will see yellow dust-like pollen fall from the flowers.

Wild apples

When you are walking by a hedgerow in the autumn, you might spot some small crab apples on the ground. Look up and you will probably see a crab-apple tree heavily laden with fruit.

Hedgerow flowers

If you walk alongside a hedgerow in spring and summer, it won't just be trees that you see. Keep your eyes peeled, and you will spot wild flowers just about everywhere you look.

Fantastic foxgloves

Foxgloves are often grown in gardens, but you can also see them growing wild in hedgerows and woodlands. If you look closely, you will see patterns of dots on the petals. The dots guide bees towards the nectar, which is deep inside the flowers. When the bees crawl in, their bodies become covered in pollen.

Spreading foxgloves

Foxgloves spread easily because each flower spike produces thousands of seeds. When the seeds are ripe, they fall to the ground and, if conditions are right, they will **germinate** and grow into new foxglove plants.

Frothy cow parsley

You are probably familiar with cow parsley. Frothy clouds of these pretty flowers decorate British hedgerows from April to June.

You can recognise cow parsley (below) by its lacy white blooms.

With their tall, upright flower spikes and pink, tube-shaped flowers, foxgloves (above) are easy to spot.

Brambles are one of the easiest plants to find in a hedgerow. You will see their rose-like flowers all summer long.

Prickles and thorns

Some plants, such as blackberries, roses and thistles, have sharp thorns or spines. These stop animals from eating their leaves and stems.

Scrambling brambles
Brambles, or blackberry plants, scramble everywhere, sometimes smothering everything in their path. Towards the end of summer, the blackberry fruits ripen, turning from green to purply-black.

Hedgerow harvest
Have you ever picked juicy ripe blackberries from a hedgerow? Blackberries are probably the most delicious of all hedgerow fruits. Birds and small **mammals** love to feast on them, too. The fruits contain seeds, which pass through the animals' bodies and come out in their droppings. Wherever the seeds land, a new bramble may grow.

Dog rose
The sweet-scented dog rose is one of the prettiest hedgerow flowers of all. In the autumn, look for its bright red fruits, called hips.

Dog roses have simple pale pink blooms in the early summer and shiny hips in autumn.

Blackberries are an important source of food for small animals, such as this harvest mouse.

Deciduous woodland

In deciduous woods, you will find some of Britain's best-loved trees, from the giant oak to the slender silver birch.

The mighty oak

With their wide-spreading branches and huge trunks, oak trees are among the most impressive of all British trees. You will easily recognise their leaves by their wavy edges, which have deep indents called lobes.

Oak trees (below) grow to about 20 m in height from little acorns (right).

Common ash

You will be able to identify an ash tree by its leaves. They are divided into pairs of leaflets with a single leaflet at the tip. In late summer and autumn, look out for bunches of 'winged' fruits.

The winged fruits of ash trees (above) contain seeds. In the autumn, they spin down from the trees and are carried long distances by the wind.

Ancient tree hunt

If you find an oak tree with a very fat trunk, it's probably extremely old. You can estimate its age by measuring around the trunk. With some friends to help you, stretch some string around the tree about 1.5 m from the ground. If the trunk measures more than 5 m, the tree is more than 300 years old. You can find out more about ancient trees on the Woodland Trust website (see page 2).

Silver birches have flaky, silver-white bark, covered with black streaks and patches. They have simple leaves, with toothed edges and pointed tips.

Graceful birches

With its distinctive bark, the silver birch is easy to identify, even in winter when there are no leaves on the trees. In spring, it has bright green leaves, which become darker during the summer. In the autumn, its leaves turn yellow and brown before falling to the ground.

Autumn colours

Have you ever wondered why leaves change colour in the autumn? Leaves contain a chemical called chlorophyll, which soaks up sunlight and makes the leaves green. The leaves use the sunlight to make food for the tree. In the autumn, when the days get shorter and there is less sunlight, the chlorophyll breaks down. This makes the green colour disappear, so we can see the other colours that are in the leaves.

Beautiful beeches

The beech is one of the tallest broadleaved trees in Britain, growing to 40 m tall or more. It has smooth, grey bark and wide-spreading branches. In the autumn, its leaves turn yellow and then a rich, reddish brown.

One of the best times to see beech trees is in the autumn, when their leaves carpet the woodland floor.

Woodland flowers

When you go for a walk in the woods, don't just look at the trees. Woodlands are one of the best places to spot wild flowers, especially in the spring and summer.

Seasonal spectacles

Many flowers appear in deciduous woodland in early spring before the leaves have come out on the trees. In late spring and summer, you will only find flowers that can grow in light shade, such as violets. In the autumn and winter, look out for the yellow-green flowers of ivy.

Pale primroses

Some flowers appear in the woods surprisingly early in the year. You might find clumps of pretty, pale yellow primroses blooming in February. Look closely and you will see each flower has five delicate petals.

Wood anemones

If there is an old, deciduous wood near to where you live, a good time to visit is in March. If you are lucky, you will see starry white wood anemones covering the woodland floor. Wood anemones spread very slowly, with new plants growing up from the roots, rather than from seeds.

Primrose flowers rise up from clumps of wrinkled leaves.

If you see large patches of wood anemones, the woodland you are in has probably existed for hundreds of years.

British bluebells have flowers that droop down from one side of the stem, with petals that curl up at the tip.

Bluebell woods

Carpets of bluebells are most often found in ancient woodlands. There are over 1,000 bluebell woods in Britain. You can find one near you by checking the website of the Woodland Trust (see page 2).

Nodding bluebells

It is worth making a special trip to the woods in April and May just to see the thick carpets of shimmering bluebells. One of the first things you will notice is their incredible sweet scent.

Wild garlic

You might be able to smell ramsons or wild garlic flowers before you see them. They are from the same family of plants as the garlic that is used in cooking. Look for these pretty white flowers in damp, shady areas of the woods.

Wild garlic often grows in the same woods as bluebells.

Coniferous trees

Have you ever walked through a wood full of tall, evergreen conifers? Cool and shady, with deep carpets of fallen needles and a sweet scent of pine in the air, conifer forests are wonderful places to explore.

Trees for timber

Most of the conifer woods you see in Britain have been planted for their **timber**. Many of these trees are not **native** British species, but have been introduced from other countries. Once the trees have grown, they are chopped down and the straight trunks are sawn up into planks.

Tallest trees

If you stand at the base of a Douglas fir tree, it can be hard to see to the top! It is one of the tallest trees growing in Britain. If you can reach the needle-like leaves, feel how soft they are and smell their sweet, fruity scent.

Fallen needles

Like most other conifers, Douglas firs are evergreen trees. Instead of shedding all their leaves in the autumn, they shed their needles all through the year and constantly grow others to take their place.

Record holder

The tallest tree in Britain is a Douglas fir tree growing near Inverness, Scotland. It is over 66 m tall.

Douglas firs are members of the pine family of trees. They often grow to more than 50 m tall and can live for over 1,000 years.

These are the cones of the sitka spruce (left). When they are fully ripe, they open to release their seeds.

Conifer cones

When you are exploring a conifer forest, look out for cones on the trees and on the ground. Conifer cones are often green at first, and gradually turn brown as they ripen.

Ancient yews

Yew trees are a native British species, and the longest living trees in Britain. The most ancient of all British yews is thought to be over 5,000 years old. It is growing in a churchyard in Wales.

Yew trees often have very fat, knobbly trunks.

Yew trees can often be seen growing in parks. You can recognise them by their red berry-like cones, called arils (above).

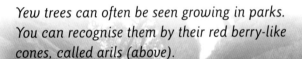

Beware!

Do not touch any part of a yew tree. Its leaves, bark and seeds are all highly poisonous!

Fields of flowers

There is nowhere quite like a wild flower meadow in summer. The ground is thick with flowers and the air is humming with insects. If you visit one, see how many different wild flowers you can spot.

Yellow buttercups
You are sure to be familiar with buttercups. Meadow buttercups (top right) are the tallest kind you will find. The flowers have five shiny petals and bloom all summer long.

Orchids
Wild orchids are easier to find in Britain than you might think. You will know common spotted orchids (bottom right) by their cone-shaped flower spikes and the purple spots on their leaves.

Wild flower wonderlands

For thousands of years, wild flower meadows have been used for making hay and for grazing farm animals such as cattle. These meadows are fantastic habitats for a huge variety of flowers, including vetch, clover and yellow-rattle. Sadly, in recent years many wild flower meadows have disappeared, and the land is now used for growing **crops**.

Snakeshead fritillaries

With their checked lantern-like flowers, snakeshead fritillaries are among the most beautiful of all wild flowers in Britain. If you are lucky, you might find some growing in a damp meadow in spring.

Perfect poppies

With their bright red petals and black centres, poppies are unmistakable. You can sometimes see them in great numbers in cornfields where the crop has not been sprayed with weed-killing chemicals.

Poppy profusion

Some wild flowers live for many years, but poppies are annuals, which means they only live for a year. Each plant produces up to a hundred flowers in a summer. All the flowers produce lots of seeds, so new poppies can grow year after year.

A field full of bright red poppies is one of the great wild flower sights of the summer.

Snakeshead fritillaries have become a rare sight in the wild in recent years.

Flowers on farms

Some farmers deliberately leave space for wild flowers to grow around the edge of their fields. These strips of land, which are not sprayed with chemicals to kill weeds or insects, provide an important habitat for flowers such as brilliant blue cornflowers. Once a common sight in fields, these pretty wild flowers are now rarely found in Britain.

Rivers, streams and ponds

Wherever you live in Britain, you probably have a river, stream or pond nearby. If you explore these habitats, you will discover a rich variety of trees and wild flowers that grow well in damp or wet soil.

Flowering alder

Alder trees can often be seen growing near to rivers and streams. Look out for clusters of flowers hanging down from the branches. These are called catkins. They are the tree's male flowers. Like many trees, the alder has separate male and female flowers.

Kingcups

In the spring and summer, golden yellow marsh marigolds, or kingcups, light up the edges of rivers, streams and ponds with luxurious colour. These are among the most ancient of all native British plants.

If you spot some kingcups, notice the cup-shaped flowers and the glossy, dark green leaves.

If you see some male alder catkins, look carefully and you might see some of the small, egg-shaped female catkins, too.

Female catkin
Male catkin

Seeds on water

An alder tree's female catkins are pollinated by pollen from the long, dangling male catkins. They gradually become fruits that look like small, woody cones. When they are ripe, they open to release their seeds, which are carried away by the wind and the water.

Yellow flags

You will often find yellow irises, or yellow flags, growing along riverbanks or at the edge of ponds. Notice their long, sword-shaped leaves and bright yellow flowers. Their sweet scent is very attractive to bees.

Crack willows

One of the trees you are most likely to see on a riverbank is a crack willow. You can recognise them by their long, narrow leaves. They have slender, flexible stems, which have traditionally been used for making baskets.

Cracking name

The wood of crack willows is quite fragile, and twigs and branches often break off. The cracking sound they make is what gives the trees their name.

Crack willows (below) can grow to a height of 25 m, but they are often kept shorter by being cut back, or 'pollarded'. This causes lots of new branches to grow.

Yellow flags (above) are common throughout Britain. You can see them flowering towards the end of May.

Heaths and moors

Moors and heaths are large areas of open land where the soil is poor and few trees grow. Plants need to be tough to survive the windswept conditions here, but there are many wild flower treasures to find.

Strange sundew

Look at the glistening droplets of liquid on this round-leaved sundew plant (right). They look a bit like dew or raindrops, but in fact they are very sticky. When an insect lands on a leaf, it gets stuck. The leaf then curls up and traps the insect inside. The plant then **digests** the insect and **absorbs** its nutrients.

Purple hills

A good time to visit a heath or moor is in late summer. This is when heather, or ling, comes into flower, turning whole hillsides purple and pink. If you see some heather, try to get up close to smell the delicate, honey-scented flowers.

Heather has tough, woody stems that grow low to the ground to protect the plant from the wind.

Round-leaved sundews (above) cannot get enough nutrients from the poor soil on heaths and moors, so they feed on insects, too!

In the mountains

You will need to take some warm clothes when you look for trees and wild flowers in the mountains. Even in the summer, strong, cold winds can make this a harsh environment. But it will be worth the trip.

Mountain trees

In the mountains, trees are only able to grow below a certain height, called the **treeline**. Higher up, conditions are too harsh and the air is too cold. One of the most magnificent trees you will see in the mountains is the Scots pine. With its orange-brown bark and blue-green needles, it is one of the prettiest of all conifers.

Mountain flowers

Even above the treeline, you will find colourful flowers brightening up the landscape. Many mountain flowers, such as moss campion, grow low to the ground to protect themselves from harsh winds.

You can see bright clumps of moss campion flowering in spring on cliffs and mountainsides in Wales, Scotland and northern England.

Scots pines are native conifers that live for up to 700 years and grow to a height of 35 m.

Weather warning

Always take some warm, waterproof clothing when you walk in the mountains, as the weather can change very quickly. Go with an adult and let someone know details of where you are going and when you expect to return.

Seaside flowers

With strong winds and salty air, conditions by the sea are tough for plants. The wild flowers that grow here all have special features to help them survive.

Cliff-top colour

In autumn and winter, a walk along a coastal path can be bleak and cold. But in the spring and summer, the cliff tops burst into colour with carpets of dazzling flowers. One of the plants you are most likely to see is pretty sea pink, or thrift.

Thrift is often battered by sea winds, so it has extra long roots to anchor it firmly in the ground.

Drifts of thrift

You can recognise thrift by its grass-like leaves and pink flower heads that look like lollipops.

Safety first

When you are walking along a coastal trail, always keep to the path and stay well away from the edge of the cliffs.

*Look out for sea holly growing on grassy **sand dunes**.*

Prickly holly

You can't mistake sea holly for any other flower. You will know it by its prickly silvery leaves and egg-shaped, blueish flower heads.

Waxy leaves

Like many plants that grow near the sea, sea holly has leaves that are covered in a thick, waxy coating. This helps to keep water in and protects them from the harsh, salty air.

Sea bindweed

Trailing among the grass on the sand dunes, you may also find some sea bindweed. These large, pink-and-white stripy flowers are easy to recognise. Sea bindweed grows low to the ground and, like thrift, it has long roots that stop it from being blown away.

Sea bindweed has flowers that are shaped a bit like the end of a trumpet.

In the garden

You might think the flowers and trees you see in gardens are very different from those that are found in the wild. But some of our best-loved garden plants come originally from wild species that have existed in Britain for thousands of years.

Cultivated cousins

Have you ever seen foxgloves or primroses growing in a garden? If so, they were probably not wild flowers, but varieties that had been deliberately produced, or 'cultivated', from native wild species.

Colourful cranesbills

You will see cranesbills, or geraniums, growing in gardens all over Britain. They are the cultivated relatives of wild cranesbills, which you can find growing along country lanes and in meadows.

Pretty pasque flowers

Pasque flowers (below), or pulsatillas, are among the rarest of all British wild flowers, but you can often see cultivated varieties growing in gardens. If you want to find them in the wild, look in dry meadows and on hillsides.

You can recognise pasque flowers by their bright yellow centres and feathery leaves.

If you see a cranesbill in flower, there are sure to be bees buzzing about! Bees are very attracted to their purple petals.

Mountain ash

It should be easy to spot mountain ash trees in your neighbourhood. People often grow them in their front gardens. Their flowers are an excellent source of nectar for bees and their berries are irresistible to birds. In the wild, they grow in mountainous parts of Scotland.

Orchard trees

Fruit trees are fantastic plants to grow in a garden. The apple, plum and cherry trees grown in orchards and gardens have all been developed from species that grow in the wild.

With its pretty blossom in spring and delicious fruit in the autumn, an apple tree is the ideal tree to grow in a garden.

Like a common ash (see page 14), the mountain ash (above) has leaves that are divided into lots of leaflets. From late summer, its berries provide a tasty treat for thrushes and other birds.

A home in the trees

Garden trees provide food and shelter for many kinds of animals. In spring and summer, insects feast on their flowers and birds nest in their branches. In the autumn and winter, their fruits provide food for hungry birds and for mammals such as squirrels, hedgehogs and foxes.

Finding trees and wild flowers

You don't need to be an expert to enjoy trees and wild flowers. Here are a few tips that might help you identify some of the less well-known species you spot.

Handy items

A notebook and pen is useful for making notes about the trees and flowers you see. If you have a camera, it can be helpful to take photographs. You can use a **field guide** to identify the plants and find out more about them.

Flower clues

Every species of wild flower is different, but they all have clues that will help you identify them. Look carefully at the colour, shape, number and size of the petals. Notice the shape of the leaves, too. Jot down these details in your notebook, along with the date and the place where the flower is growing. You should then be able to find the flower in a field guide.

Tree clues

The more you notice about a tree, the easier it will be to identify. Are the leaves wide and flat or are they tough, narrow needles? Are they simple or compound? What colour is the bark? Is it bumpy or smooth? You might also find clues such as nuts on the ground.

With eight to twelve bright yellow petals and heart-shaped leaves, lesser celandines are easy to identify. You will spot them growing in shady woodlands, along roadsides and in damp meadows in spring.

If you find some nuts with spiny cases that are split into four, you will know you are standing under a beech tree.

Classification of trees and flowers

To understand plants and animals, scientists look at their similarities and differences and sort them into groups. This is called classification.

Grouping plants and animals

Animals are divided into those with backbones (vertebrates) and those without backbones (invertebrates). Plants are divided into those that make seeds and those that do not make seeds, such as algae, mosses and ferns. Flowers and trees belong to the group of plants that make seeds.

Grouping seed-bearing plants

Seed-bearing plants are divided into two groups, or classes – flowering plants and non-flowering plants.

Seed bearing plants

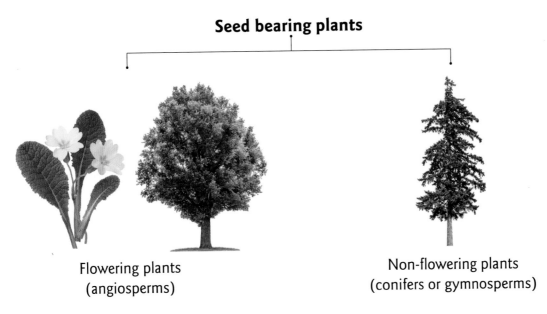

Flowering plants
(angiosperms)

Non-flowering plants
(conifers or gymnosperms)

From class to species

Flowering plants and non-flowering plants are further divided into smaller groups called orders. The orders are divided into families. There are around 415 families of flowering plant and eight families of conifer. Families are further divided into genera. Species are the smallest groups – they are types of flowers and trees that are so similar that they **reproduce** together.

Glossary

absorbs takes in or soaks up

ancient hedgerow a hedgerow that has existed for around 300 years or more

broadleaved trees trees with wide, flat leaves

cones the fruits of conifers

conifers trees that bear cones

crops plants grown in fields for food

deciduous of a tree that loses its leaves in the autumn

digests breaks down into substances that can be used

evergreen having green leaves all year round

field guide a book used for identification

fruits the parts of a plant that contain its seeds

germinate to begin to grow

habitat a place where animals or plants live

identify to discover what something is

mammals animals that give birth to live young and feed them with their own milk

native of an animal or plant that has existed in a particular country for thousands of years

nectar a sweet liquid produced by flowers

needles the narrow leaves of conifer trees

nutrients substances that keep plants alive

pollen a fine yellow powder made by flowers

pollinate to put pollen into a flower so it develops fruit and seeds

reproduce to produce offspring

sand dunes mounds of sand formed by the wind

seed a tiny part of a plant that can grow into a new plant

seed heads the heads of flowers when they contain seeds

shrub a woody plant that is smaller than a tree

species a type of animal or plant that breeds with others of the same kind

stems the main central parts of plants

timber wood used for making things

treeline the height above which no trees grow

weeds wild plants that grow where they are not wanted

Index